Mindfield

A Poetry Collection

JASPER RIPLEY

INFERNO PRESS

Copyright © 2025 Jasper Ripley

All rights reserved. No part of this book may be reproduced, distributed, or transmitted in any form or by any means, electronic or mechanical, including photocopying, recording, or by any information storage and retrieval system — without prior written permission from the author, except for brief quotations used in reviews or scholarly works.

This work may not be used in whole or in part for the development, training, or input of artificial intelligence systems, text and data mining, or other similar technologies.

Photo by Susan Wilkinson

Cover design & illustration by Jasper Ripley

First Edition

Published by Inferno Press

Vancouver, British Columbia

For inquiries: info.infernopress@gmail.com

INFERNO
PRESS

ISBN (paperback) 978-1-0698273-0-2

ISBN (ebook) 978-1-0698273-1-9

Printed in Canada/the United States of America

For the brave, the gone, and my mom.

Everything that deceives may be said to enchant.

— Plato

Contents

Preface · xii

I

All Eyes on Me	2
Little Orestes	4
Birthday	5
Devilish Dilemmas	6
The Forest Dance	7
Victims of Volunteer	8
Old Friends	9
You Are What You Eat	10
Latency	11
A Man of My Word	12
Temptations	14
Color of the Week	15
Guilty Conscience	16
Defuse	17
She-Devil in the Wild	18
Intent	21

II

The Flesh Assignment	24
Alaska	25

The Act	26
Ravenously Aware	27
Look for Us	28
Wanted: Dead or Alive	30
Patrimony	31
Quest to Become a Daemon	32
Parasites	33
Refuge	34
Timekeeper	35
The Cost of Happiness	36
Death by Strangulation	38
Assets	39
The Field	40
Growing Pains	41
Hotwire	42

III

The Chameleon	46
Border Child	47
The Breakdown of an Ego	48
Emeritus Devil	49
Sympathizer	50
The Invisible Man	51
Buoyant	52
Unforgivable	54

Equality for Monsters	55
The War of Attrition	56
Learning to Walk	57
Young Love in the Aftermath	58
On My Bedside Table	60
Symbiotic with the Enemy	61
Counter-Victimization 101	62
Violets	64
Half Naked and Almost Human	65

IV

Persecution	68
Immortal Souls with Mortal Attitudes	69
Peace, At Last	70
The Night Doesn't Lie	71
The Curse of Chrome Skin	72
Bad Habits	73
The Last Train	74
Ranger	77
Top of the Food Chain	78
Et Tu, Brute?	79
The City That Never Sleeps	80
Purgatory	81
In Your Will	82
Transient	83

Qualia	84
Cherished	86
In Memory Of...	87

Notes	89
Soundtrack & Playlist	90
About the Author	91

Preface

For all my life, I've lived in paradoxes that have propelled me through a turbulent youth. The minefield of my mind, was a divergent yet treacherous place— it held memories, beliefs and desires I was always at war with.

These unspoken thoughts have plagued my mind since childhood, embodying two opposites in every turn of life. They wreaked constant havoc concealed, until I set them free through these poems.

Written in these pages is the aftermath of channeling inner conflict into new perspectives the year I turned eighteen.
Now, at nineteen, I offer this collection as a reflection of both the realizations I had then, and the evolving intentions that have guided me since, in my pursuit of something more transcendent.

This collection unfolds in four movements (I–IV). It charts stages and embodiments of recurring conflict, delivered through different dimensions of evolution— including identity, morality, ego, grief, loss and regret. Through battles lost, won, and ongoing, I untangle past trauma, expand in philosophy, and discover a higher purpose.

This is not a collection that will heal you. But it may offer you another perspective on life, its impermanence, and allow you a deeper understanding of what drives those who act from inner conflict. For those who recognize themselves in these pages, may this set you free.

For readers who wish to explore *Mindfield* in another dimension, an accompanying soundtrack follows this collection as a sonic extension of its themes and reflections. It is available in the end section, under "**Soundtrack & Playlists**". You may choose to listen as you read for an immersive experience, or afterward, as a reflective journey through what you've completed.

If you wish to listen while reading, you may begin the soundtrack now.

I

All Eyes on Me

they keep staring
at my doubled eyes,
no,
lies,
they can't see me, can they?

faces pale against the window,
i see them, loud and clear with
the fog spilling out secrets.

peer through the glinting convex,
panic rushes the chandelier in
pitch black elation.

tiptoe to spell out
d e s p e r a t e
now they plea, for a deplorable light—
midday's imposter.

the moon and i
have a vendetta,
we play the invisible game.

they think they hide,
bite their tongues,
ribs shaking and tides high,

i think they're in denial.

no, they can't see me.
but they know i'm here.

Little Orestes

looks up at mom,
like driftwood,
his heart, in honesty.

eyes iridescent,
now wide in sparkling fright.

all he ever wanted,
to be a lone wishing tree,
stand tall against roaring seas,
an anchor for the mothership.

but at some point,
his mooring line
grew serpentine,
deep sea desires
now intertwined.

all that he tried,
could not debark
his tainted heart,
for saplings of evil still flourished,
in a greenhouse of love.

BIRTHDAY

at the gates of my childhood,
the devil visited me.
i stood at a precipice, quietly
admiring my last dusk.

my visitor is a prophet,
he foretells the breakdown of an ego.
i am told that it's my time
to become heir to my true face,

when the sun comes out at dawn,
i'll be all grown up,
with mismatched wings,
and a specious grin.

i shook hands with him, and walked the other way
to outrun the sun, betrayed by the retrograde.

the next morning, flowers had wilted
blue skies were now a dull grey,
he sent a crow, pecking at the windowsill
asking for my birthday.

Devilish Dilemmas

devils with angel faces,
how convenient it is
to merge with seamless ease.
to enjoy the graces of conformity,
to revel at boundless heights.

how demeaning it is,
for the non conformist soul
to be rendered acquiescent
to be desired for your pretense
to be taken for what you loathe most.

THE FOREST DANCE

one step to the left,
one to the right,
careful not to wake
each napping leaf.

the forest is my accomplice,
it's out of your control.
ballerinas from the sky,
pirouette to weigh you down.

do you feel, the coldness of the night?
the only rebels are the stars.

in the woods you must sway
around dutiful raindrops,
and even then you're amidst
a conspiracy for the great escape.

don't you get away now,
don't be so frantic.
you don't realize yet,
the night itself is mercy.

Victims of Volunteer

my latest infatuation,
why won't you cry?

persephone,
i delegate
all my teardrops
to go after your wounds,
hunt you down
in a manic frenzy,
what a thrill the chase is.

like all good things,
you must come to an end.

look at you,
pridefully treading
over heaping bodies.
think of a different fate,
you worship new religions.

how enchanting it would be,
to feel desire for mercy,
just one chip of remorse.

Old Friends

for a lifetime,
we've been keeping
each other's secrets,
keeping
each other secret,

you've reduced your appetite
to mere bloodlust.
what have you become?
now that destiny
offends your insolence.

i'm just starting to wonder,
if you finally remember me.

You Are What You Eat

everyone covets the eternal sunshine,
yet none alive with a spotless mind.

summon the devil,
the devil is free.
they'd sell their souls
to me for beauty,

but it's just a routine,
i keep telling them,
a paranoia
of the neurotic sort.

but every time,
i barely suppress my laughter,
feeling corners of my mouth
tug into duplicitous smiles.

who knew?
the secret to youth,
is a carnivorous diet
of human hearts.

LATENCY

i'm making decisions,
i am.
making
bad
decisions,

i'm not
not.
not gonna give up,

until i'm making decisions,
i am.
not

A Man of My Word

inevitable and imminent,
my shadow looms over you
like shrouds of raincloud.

pooling at your feet,
the downpour of acid rain
begins to sear vain mouths,
scarring lips of embrace.

faltering voices,
i catch my breath.
your mascara runs red
at the slightest caress,

a peace offering.
so you ask me,
what i'm thinking
in moments like this.

my willpower eludes me.
all i can do is stop and stare,
counting words that you've lost,
between gaps in your teeth...

each shiver redeems

a rolling stone,

by way of siphoning

deep into vortices

of midnight cravings.

my word is my bond,

i will not wither you.

i bet, you didn't know that

i always have the chance

to start all over again.

Temptations

hello, vermin of earth.

i'll wait for you,

to excavate your colony.

it feels like, i'm my best around you,

but you draw out the worst in me.

i can't take the animals out of you,

but you always take the watcher out of me.

Color of the Week

she lives,
in between the gaps of weekdays.

each pocket of vibrant air
prepares her for reaping,

merciless mondays,
she wears indecision.
adorned by passionate shades
of green and of purple.

friday's taxation,
rung her dry, streaked,
and worn down face,
ten years older in seven days.
she's grayscale and still
weathering,
withering.

so eager to be fated,
she's a star crossed lover.
forever and always,
painted by the altar.

Guilty Conscience

don't look at me.
unlike you,
i have nothing tethering me
to the bleak underworld.

but you,
mortal,
deep in your soul
you know,
deep under your feet,

hell is your traveling house
draped in the upside down
when you'd rather be on the platter,
than feed and forgive yourself.

Defuse

the art of provocation
is a three step process:

the show,
the hunt,
the sabotage.

it was my job to know you,
without you knowing me.
now it's my job to convince you
that i am something i'm not.

trip over a provoked time bomb,
rewind your actions to defuse.

set it off,
alarm to wake the still.
in due time,
shellshocked out of place.

disarm me,
you only need to take away my face
but all i want, is you.

She-Devil in the Wild

it's been 176 days,
since i last saw my reflection.
not even Dr. Etheridge, could
pull me into the physical.

on thursday, i stepped into her office,
i looked at her eyes, they
smiled at mine
but with all her might,
she still looked
right through me.

it's been 5 months, since you and i
first shared a glance through the fourth wall,

No.

i am sealed,
against your effervescence.

i'm only used to ephemera,
like something beached
then stranded at sea again.

we read each other,
by faulty lines
on our sides, crumpled
in sweaty palms,

you lean in, and
i can only retreat
with aloofness,
like an owl, frozen
to peripherals.

now we're pretending, like the slow burn
across the room isn't gnawing at our bones,

your stare
is drilling holes
into my jugular.

perforations, like
the grenade to
explode in blonde.

Jasper Ripley

i'm really struggling,
with the color blonde.

why don't you see through me?
and fail like doctors' tears.

though you're only treasured
by gullible eyes,

i know, i should entertain
our month long chess game,
you're enticing and that,
is why i must end it here.

INTENT

sees tears of joy
drizzled over first breaths,

and those of despair
pouring at one's last.

you've misunderstood
the forbidden fruit.
it's no temptation, no deception,

only the ticket
to a piteous loop
of soothing the same old laceration,
engraved into our bones.

who is the devil, really?
am i a sole punisher
as the punished i am?

dad, i've deciphered
your original sin.

II

THE FLESH ASSIGNMENT

listen to the boy who cried wolf,
for he knows the hue of remorse
that trickles down verdancy.

in the mirror, look for the stranger,
for you will be in metamorphosis,
and emerge beside perishables.

Alaska

when i fell,
i was so gilded
i thought the forest
rushed up to meet me.

sizzle, chanted,
the rope in protest.
but the wind whistled,
overjoyed, to witness downfall.

in between breaths of regret,
i fear
i feel
there is an evil here,
that cannot be described,
only felt.

The Act

this dreary night,
under the cover of darkness,
i scale walls to reach you,

i tranquilize you,

i catch you,

there i hold you.
your body intact and still,
your heart unbroken.

the stakes are high,
i set you down
so the sky won't swallow you,
but even i can't hold steady now.

Ravenously Aware

beautiful healer,
seek me,
i need morphine
and you to ration.

celestial wisdom,
enlighten me,
i need a revelation
to speak with grandmasters.

big brother,
extort me,
i'll need a confession
after i dose my healer.

Look for Us

like rodents, we scurry
underground,
fearful of the open sky.

we are the blind spots
in spinning cylinders
of warm revolvers.

i bet with my life,
in games we play
against death in Vegas,

it's not who i am.

you'll remember us only
by one in hundreds, of
meaningless names.

crawling in plain sight,
but you never see us,
until papers outlive
our bloodlines.

we are the ghosts
who become you,
when you die.

i'll take care of your name,
so please take care of us
while we're alive.

WANTED: DEAD OR ALIVE

when i find myself
in the crosshairs,
dead or alive, i know
there is a star
embossed in my name.

we're prized because we come and go,

cover me with the freedom blanket,
lay the stripes over my dark oak torso,
carry me to walk my last
but remember me as i lived,

i do not consent to the interests of my ▮
i do not ▮ to my handler
i do ▮ consent
▮ do not
i

Patrimony

in this tragedy,
the lineage holds us hostage.

so much poise, hiding
beneath a titanium shell
with dents and scratches,
stacked like rings, tell
next winter to give birth.

so many vultures, circling
above an enduring crown,
with a carcass called the body.
bruises chronicle her journal,
in January, they stand as testimonies.

so, all-seeing souls,
did evil begin
with fifteen volts,
or in the womb?

Quest to Becoming a Daemon

i can only survive
suspended
in interstice, where i am
invisible
to piercing eyes,
invincible
to the shame of time.

will i ever be invited
to roam the earth
indifferent to the vessel i pilot
ingrained,
bequeath my bones to someone
who will cherish them.

i must live in interludes,
only there, shall i be free,
eternally confined.

Parasites

burrow in my mind,
spread verity unspoken.
i can feel these tendrils
reaching for me,

firing nerves, pollute
the air i cannot draw.
enshroud my mouth,
hesitate for iron lungs.

this host breaks in half,
for worlds
Alexander cannot save.
but the cure,
is only within patient zero.

Refuge

the condemned
always run from condemnation
like it could ever be escaped,

encased,
the condensation of breathless vows
outpaces thunder,
envelops the fairest minefields.

wayfarers, i've been aiding you
in your hitchhike to the promised land
far too long to keep you concealed.

judgment will uncover the retreat,
and when it does,
earth won't be
for humans only.

Timekeeper

riding the bus,
alongside my slumped posture

dangling on the minute hand,
a cynical man
blames the shoelaces
for the breaking dam,

tick
*toc*k

now pressed to my temple,
counting each second.
the passage of unrealized gold
is the fortune he hoards,

the pendulum swings,
he does not learn,
nor leave, nor wait.

The Cost of Happiness

in how many lifetimes, have we met?
in every life,
am i equally scared of first death
because you are alive?

you're killing me
again and again,
you obfuscate my purpose,

but we're fading,
rapid as tears.
you were also born
the day that i was.

as magnets, we repel and resist
through the silence,
through the tunnels,
we are still tethered.

you're only wrapping the cord tighter,
my lifeline slowly going pale,
it's tangled and knotted now.

people say we only live once,
find what brings us happiness,
so honor what gives us truth.

dear mom, the other half of my happiness
lies in *you*.

Death by Strangulation

strings, bring me to sleep.
i'm restless,
in a carriage of casted blight.
my gifts can only withstand decades
of the all-consuming, centurial rot,

it comes to barricade my hunger
as i once forbade destinies,

time, take me to resurrection.
allow me to wake,
in a casket of inception.

Assets

hope.
a word entirely foreign.
it was a soft word
so naturally,
it didn't exist in our vocabulary.

it implied the possibility of a future,
reverse the clamor of cold steel.
an alternate ending to trepidation,
was this all our duty meant?

the anticipation is killing me,
how dare *hope* spoil the suspense.

don't it dare,
offer us an easy way out.
can't imagine,
the cowardice in this word.
god forbid,
it became a part of our vernacular,

i hope we survive this one.

THE FIELD

glacial eyes,

stare me down.

sable hair,

veil my pain.

storied blood,

cure my plight.

labored breath,

steady my aim.

Growing Pains

youth
came in the form of women,
who swore to undo twisted fate
and bring closure to watchful eyes.

age
came in the form of wonder,
which swore to indebt me with wealth
and bring grief to knowing lies.

Hotwire

i never wanted to find us here,
you and i in the hot seats.

remember when
the world was in our hands,
you were the brown wire
in every car we hotwired.

ignite,
to jumpstart my heartbeat
for the fourth time.

before we outgrew
our happily ever after,
remember how we lay
sprawled on diner tables,

painkillers numbing all our senses.

crossing the circuits to jolt
cold-engined immaturity, hurry.
it puts everything in perspective, death.
what is worth adoring without an end?

on the bridge
with reckless high beams,
you were the master key
to all the lovers' padlocks.

back then
we tried to be kids.
we were twelve,
and we were sixty.

erase everything we knew,

nothing can protect me.
not another body,
not another name,

my life has been a facade
except the lilacs in your hair.
those, i handpicked.
would you call that grand theft?

III

The Chameleon

pigment flowing down the branches,
staining the oldest resident rainbow.

the vertical river cascades,
varnishing riven bark,
repainting the foliage.

in a cradle of woven leaves,
the chameleon lies bare,
bleeding new colors,
unwrapped at last.

its dry mouth crackles like firewood,
and speaks to the jungle:

i stand before you,
tainted and tattered with sin
i skinned myself,
now i can no longer blend in.

Border Child

i grew up in diaspora,
my heart miles away from my body,
and my body too far gone to belong.

i was always too blue,
my sand-soaked boots
dragged my hometown with me
across borders of radio silence.

this is my seventh home,
i have brothers and sisters
all around me, and above.
i send letters and bullets
to my favorite wall of stars.

impatience among dunes,
a perilous combination
with sin city sensations,
it's no way to keep naivety.

tomorrow, i move again,
the next warfront needs me.

The Breakdown of an Ego

jailed birds
erupt in defiance,
with the phantoms of
phoenices
down hallways of a fortress,
blistering with rage.

a moat surrounds,
brewing with insults.
ash-dipped walls
barely standing tall,

they don't know,
behind these scorched doors,
i lie amidst frigid cold.

halt the equilibrium
of my iniquitous soul
and suit in decomposition.

still, i catch fire,
now burning inside out
as i try to salvage the pending good.

EMERITUS DEVIL

swift and still, you melt
into shapes of repose.

rejuvenated,
you indulge a brand new day
like you forgot all about
the paradise,
that harbored you in those eight hours.

but long before you woke,
i sat in the dead of night

watching your sleep,
my leathery wings
draped over the egress.

with profane hands, i prayed,

may the worlds you travel through,
be far apart, from hells that i traverse.
may your fate always be as pure
as my intentions to surrender.

Sympathizer

the dunes have bored an arid soul,
my heart has cloned itself in whole:
a sympathizer,
it writes ballads by woeful shows,
dances deft in charming glow.

it's got all the worldly sirens fooled,
don't mistake the mess for rule.
this twin's only but a trickster,
it plays ploys to swindle her,

lives enough to befriend the wild,
barren lands turned grand plateaus.
the heart's still full of pride to spare,
here's one secret, for you to know,

for a conman that's born and raised
in the backlands of do or die,
there are things that never change
like the urge to tell a lie.
by pitiful tales, spinned or framed
it's no wonder, they're estranged.

The Invisible Man

respire,
i breathed their vitality
two faced,
and grief stricken,
i return to the X
with a wavering skeleton,
double jeopardy,
charged and tried in absentia.
rain on me,
i ask of you
to make me seen again.

Buoyant

when all we have is time,
it's all we don't have.

if only i could stall the avalanche,
desiccate it, in the drought
that has been adolescence.

journey to sulk by the cove,
my wings are dark with thirst
but i'm rooted in the glaciers,
toss and turn but i cannot drown.

blizzards surge in my stomach,
this unrest will live vicariously
in hounds hungry for spotlight.

what is an orchard in wasteland?
surviving gestures of bloom, rebirth
not to be stifled.
what is blood when it's a desiccant?
no thicker than water, a foe of nature.

Mindfield

amidst the dead sea,
the isolation is my lifeguard.
no body of water
tenacious enough to infiltrate
thistly hearts.

passing tides indifferent
to my floatation,
and soon the monsoon
writes in place of you.

two weeks and four days
weighs on me like perpetual war,

so release me,
i no longer serve
as the anchor i used to be.

Unforgivable

eternity holds a cruel wager,
i wear a face
time cannot forgive.

i lurk only in candlelight,
and you're bewitched.

no fragment of me knows true delight,
i am only bejeweled
by the shell of humanity.

Equality for Monsters

confusing...
i <u>trace</u> around the lot,
around and <u>around</u>.

perplexing...
present are the letters, but
absent is the ground.

the asphalt, red with <u>passion</u>,
mocks the devotion you claim
in vows <u>you</u> casually speak
with two fingers crossed behind.

so many monuments of <u>betray</u>al,
cemeteries, overflowing in greed
for the liberated to still be here.

just because the great inversion
has placed <u>man's</u> worst exhibition
superior to plain omission,
after all that you've perished,
who am i to end your <u>pulse</u>?

The War of Attrition

my totality is dictated
by your approval,
drip fed and titrated
from thawing cavalries,
it remains in search
of itself,
and a dormant mortality.

but i start not to fear you,
for the knowledge i do not possess,
seeks me as much as i seek it.

Learning to Walk

courage, what a noble lie.
to be strong is nothing but injury,
with the soul and body in such disrepair,
limping, you must carry on in a battered costume.
watch the sheltered, green-eyed envy
admire your worn-down knuckles
then settle on bravery.

Young Love in the Aftermath

it's my right to be free,
hand in hand,
with the girl too good
to go like this.

she and i can't decide,
if words are worth
the trade of lives.

hand in hand,
pretend to be brave,
the hills have eyes
but we're only kids.

it's T-minus two minutes,
heating up our capillaries.

this is our call
to bury statesmen,
prepare to embrace
as partners once last.

Mindfield

the ground warns it's about to give,
like good scouts, we dive
synchronized to the rumble.

young love is fierce as murder,
rivals destiny to bring us closer.
shield you from seething silos,
unfazed by decapitated trees,

we promised to enter, hand in hand,
and still clasped together, we dive again.

see, we have all ten, though unsteady.
look back to thank the fallen ones,
their stars aligned for us again.

capture one to pluck his teeth,
the wreckage stayed to watch us kiss.

On My Bedside Table

the bandages have seen me wake
distraught in delirium,
aching for the unafraid,
fumbling to mend the cavern.

i am a lifelong consumer
of whirring machines
and flickering lights,

i look for a surgeon
in every mother i meet,

because some days,
i still find myself with bloody hands,
and one large wound, gaping
across waist-sides of my beloved.

Symbiotic with the Enemy

i get it, i do,
people just don't like to meet
things they don't understand.

i get a bad rap,
confused with others of the faintly human.
in an infestation of the tapestry,
the enemy swarms into patchwork.

masqueraders, meet extermination.
here to wipe the pests from my name,
peel the banners stuck to walls,
a thin yellow line to defamation.

must i stand with seam rippers,
across the canyon of our great divide?

caught on the pitchforks, blindsided
by false halos of polar gods.
we're angels and we're demons,
has anyone ever thought of humans?

COUNTER-VICTIMIZATION 101

it was easy
to pilfer from
banks of injustice,

typically conceited
to blame
greater bandits,

organized crime,
like synchronized swimmers,
we've been indoctrinated.
fed the lie that is justice.

misery is not unfair,
believe me, it will hunt down
the most sheltered souls,
shattered with mundanities

but, revenge does not suffice.
it's the biggest trap we spring,
and wait to see the other die.

fantasy only widens,
convincing as a fairness
built on retribution,

you long for it.
to watch a lopsided scale,
droop until it rusts

only because you've gained
a sharper nose,
a keener eye,
to spot monsters in the wild.

Violets

bloom among snakes,
morph into polaroids
and trembling keepsakes
to stay in my wallet.

on top of the monument,
we broke down and
drained our eyes
of kerosene,

but in the back of the fuselage
we let loose and breathed our last.

bolts and frames
shake, as we bolt
and frame ourselves,

all hands on deck,
shuffle the cards,
be an ace for the test.

violets, brace for impact,
i hope we find fertile soil
in our expedition to land.

Half Naked and Almost Human

back in the garden
where it all began,
i grew an apple tree
enriched by tears,

i feel feathers,
blooming from my back,
wrap around to bring me home.

stretch out, angel.
and all i can see is falling.

blinded by white,
my sails plummet.
i watch them dismember
to the bottom of seven seas.

stripped of a smokescreen,
what will i tell them now?
what sets me apart, from
creatures in New York?

Persecution

united, they banish their king
in terror of disillusionment,
a tyrant is crowned.

they'll look to him for guidance,
like he somehow knows better
than to succumb to temptations,
he will purge.

and when they find themselves powerless,
his people will hate him,
they will exile him,
and accuse him of sanity.

Immortal Souls with Mortal Attitudes

your first words,
do not fear.

you see in all angles,
all timelines,
through the past,
into the future.

you have more means
to savor glory and ruin.
i don't doubt your taste,
you see right through me.

tell me, soldier of God,
what happens to this carrier
in the nearing apocalypse?
only silence ensues,
i have an end,
you must be confounded.

i'm not afraid,
i tried to speak to you,
but you rolled your eyes,
all ten thousand of them.

Peace, at Last

in this desert
where truth runs barren,
i leave no footprints
in famished sand.

impervious to the heat,
i trek in the sun.
my body stings from daylight,
my feet ache from wear,
but my compass, still set on the voyage.

i look to my left,
there lay the bodies of souls i traded.
their limbs now lay a bridge,
their blood now pours oases.

i look to my right,
there sat most wrenching regrets.
their prospects now cloud my judgment,
their shadows now cast a premonition.

for that, i gouged my eyes,
so all i could see was inside.

The Night Doesn't Lie

under the canopy of riches,
some have sought refuge in light.
and perhaps, in ink filled spite
with restless eyes,
gazed upon the intricacy
of a weeping constellation.

but few have felt the sting of cerulean,
or the aches of crimson spells.
they've never held burning embers
in the palms of their hands,
as stars duly descend
to propose their blessings.

but i trust the night
to tell the truth,
the whole truth,
and nothing but the truth,

> *marry her,*
> *the comets lusted,*
> *so you'll be wedded*
> *in a prison*
> *of hope.*

The Curse of Chrome Skin

faster than time,
i'm flying in the slipstream.
my titanium is one, near liquid,
with the speed machine.

for a moment
i forget about my age, my face,
the half-life of my carbon heart.
i feel only stainless, alive.

i'm all the world wars incarnate,
isn't this, all that man wants?
bodies and eternal life,
foolish to want both at once.

in a second i'll have to return,
wipe the blue blood from my nose.
these days, dread permeates the planet.

to go back to genesis,
i'd give up all my memories.
it feels more like a curse,
remembering synthetics.

Bad Habits

my youth is always fleeting, like
tomorrow is the one chasing me.
i surrender gifts of precociousness,
return me before the beauty.

i wish to be sheltered
in the warmth of oblivion,
showered in decay
then basked in naivety,

i wish to be good,
i know that's a lie.
i'm coursing with ambition,
to conquer the great unknown.

but my worst habit of all,
i don't ever want to step,
and know that the ground
is going to hold me.

The Last Train

when i was a kid,
i often looked into the future
and saw my mother monochrome,
doing little things by her lonesome.

i used to collect pennies and dimes
in a glass jar to reverse our curse.
she used to believe in me like i was her,
with love, hand laid my newborn tracks,

and with juvenile teardrops, i signed
every letter damp on her pillowcase.
back then, the language of pen pals
saved us from being strangers.

it's all a roll of dice,
empty envelopes, folded stamps
with or without a return address.

but unlike me, she's no risk taker.
her travels home are only by train,
the fear of flying keeps her grounded.

i thought, there must be a mistake,
like all naive children, i bet on lady luck
to keep us close, and far from derailment.

just a decade later, i'm at our last train station.

the final train that's about to depart from here
will not come back for traveling ghosts, running
after its locomotive hum, in tardy regret...
i can't blame it on the railway,
blame it on something,

the gates, the water,
the twist of fate,
must it sentence me
the pain of imagination?

in my dreams,
time dilates while i hold her
at the platform, her stubborn scent
will linger, as long as   the guilt consumes me.

i will leave her   i will leave myself

she will hate me   she will love me

i will love me   i will hate me
and weep.   and weep.

Ranger

i am a prodigal son,
everything i do
is laced with your rebellion.

Top of the Food Chain

in all of earth's unconscious wanderers,
why are we the freedom fighters
with the least freedom?

is it the cardinal sins
or just the fear of being left behind?

is it only the price to pay
to live and die as wide-eyed beasts?

Et Tu, Brute?

lately, it seems,
every corner i turn,
i find myself hunted by prey.

front toward enemy,
the lies of my landmines
bending over backwards,

trickery is an innate gift
in the absence of caution.
wilful as treason, come find me
down in the depths of hell.

lying on the pavement,
marks indelible,
drenched in a cruel joke.

but at last, i wield open arms,
this rain washing away the sin
that's torn me from limb to limb.

this bounty is cool, calm,
and soon to be collected.

The City That Always Sleeps

streets of folded people,
does it only take a backbone
to stand up straight?
or will you always flicker,
let freedom enslave you?

and when the high finds exhale,
do you really believe
that you will be missed?
or will you lift and straighten
the spine of your homeland?

Purgatory

i've landed at the port of in-between,
the pull of two homes, is where i belong.

please stop reminding me,
that i'm a child of God,
i learned to read
in hell's half-light.

machines taught me to love,
they're halfway to heaven,
we're still caught in the divide.

yet under the veil of sanity,
i must camouflage
the doom of a hybrid.

repeat the ascent and fall,
plunge through worlds
on the cusp of judging new souls,
mine still hanging in the balance.

In Your Will

your silhouette lives on
like veins through marble.
your wit within my skull,
each endeavor burning
with a spark like yours.

Transient

to time's stamp, we barely impress.
we can only ensure, our moments here
are shaped by the truest choices.

opioids are a modern iceberg,
what if i am, too?

does it mean, i should relapse
on the hope of sobriety?

to you, i barely impress.
i'll always be a wreck,
even in oceans of wealth.

i can only hope you will love,
in some way like i'm starting to now.

Qualia

all of these faces,
little orestes.
the maniacal devil.
the wanted man.
the timekeeper.

every permutation of me
lives simultaneously,
at a quantum crossroad,
stuck in superposition.

they pull and prod
my body, compel me
to split into battalions
in dire need, to leave
some closing legacy.

but i am also the devil who confessed,
a prisoner only within confines of doubt,
and the sole keeper of my defiant hours.

the path i have taken,
seems dead set
on pelting the hourglass
with shrapnels of treachery.

i know, i've been less than good
but i think, i'm ready to multiply.

to be all that i am, i need nothing
that is not already found
from within.

Cherished

don't try to be a hero,
Arlington is full of them
and they can't even smell the flowers.

no goodbyes,
button your sleeves,
take your breath,

before you know it,
before your knees
graze the concrete,

i'm already gone.

so no goodbyes,
just savor the blink
and know that you tried.

In Memory Of...

a cancerous carnage
has taken hold of me,
i'm surviving off a repurposed heart.

my only solace,
the malleability of my madness.
may it be,
so bountiful to break my fall.

this colorless creek,
will flow like freedom.
this desolate vault,
will beat like love.

my time is finite,
no matter how much i try
to stop disrobing
into a painful consciousness.

i don't need a funeral,
not even a nice bouquet.
when i die,
i just want to be remembered.

Notes

This book's epigraph is from Plato's "The Republic".

"The Act" is inspired by a passage from Jamil Jan Kochai's short story "Playing Metal Gear Solid V: The Phantom Pain", published in the New Yorker.

"You Are What You Eat" borrows a phrase from Alexander Pope's "Eloisa to Abelard".

"Violets" is for the H's.

The title "Half Naked and Almost Human" is inspired by "Half Naked and Almost Famous", a 2012 EP by MGK.

"Cherished" includes a segment adapted from a ransom note associated with the 1980 bombing of Harvey's Resort Hotel and Casino in Stateline, Nevada. It's written in dedication and remembrance for K. E.

Soundtrack & Playlist

A soundtrack was curated as a sonic extension of *Mindfield*, following the emotional and thematic journey of the collection. You may listen as you read for an immersive experience, or afterward to revisit this journey.

Available as streaming playlists:

- Spotify

    https://open.spotify.com/playlist/5QkUsgtymVLJkseOHvNBE5

- Apple Music

    https://music.apple.com/playlist/mindfield-the-soundtrack/pl.u-r2yBDbYuPZxVPkZ

(All music remain the property of their respective artists.)

About the Author

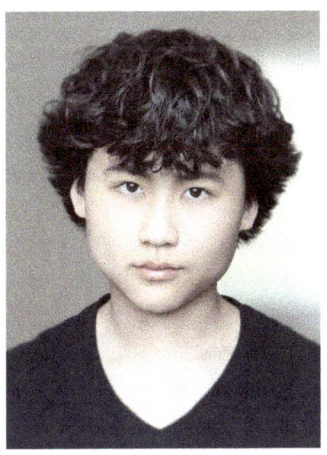

Jasper Ripley is an actor, writer and artist living in Vancouver, BC. This is his debut poetry collection, which he also designed and illustrated.

www.ingramcontent.com/pod-product-compliance
Lightning Source LLC
Chambersburg PA
CBHW052211090526
44584CB00019BA/3051